WORLD'S LONGEST-LIVING ANIMALS

200-YEAR-OLD RED SEA URCHINS!

By Topper Evans

Gareth Stevens PUBLISHING

Please visit our website, www.garethstevens.com. For a free color catalog of all our high-quality books, call toll free 1-800-542-2595 or fax 1-877-542-2596.

Cataloging-in-Publication Data

Names: Evans, Topper.
Title: 200-year-old red sea urchins! / Topper Evans.
Description: New York : Gareth Stevens Publishing, 2017. | Series: World's longest-living animals | Includes index.
Identifiers: ISBN 9781482456394 (pbk.) | ISBN 9781482455977 (library bound) | ISBN 9781482456417 (6 pack)
Subjects: LCSH: Sea urchins–Juvenile literature.
Classification: LCC QL384.E2 E93 2017 | DDC 593.9'5–dc23

Published in 2017 by
Gareth Stevens Publishing
111 East 14th Street, Suite 349
New York, NY 10003

Designer: Andrea Davison-Bartolotta and Bethany Perl
Editor: Ryan Nagelhout

Photo credits: Cover, p. 1 Aaron Nystrom/iStock/Thinkstock; pp. 2–24 (background) Dmitrieva Olga/Shutterstock.com; p. 5 Dave Wrobel/Visuals Unlimited/Getty Images; p. 7 kateukraine/Shutterstock.com; p. 9 Ingrid Maasik/Shutterstock.com; p. 11 Crystal Kirk/Shutterstock.com; p. 13 Greg Amptman/Shutterstock.com; p. 15 Seaphotoart/Shutterstock.com; p. 17 Calvin Larsen/Science Source/Getty Images; p. 19 Napat Photography/Shutterstock.com; p. 21 Stuart Westmorland/Corbis Documentary/Getty Images.

Printed in the United States of America

CPSIA compliance information: Batch #CW17GS: For further information contact Gareth Stevens, New York, New York at 1-800-542-2595.

CONTENTS

Ocean Urchins 4

Test and Spines 8

Big Red 10

Using Their Feet 12

Time to Feed 14

One Big Eye 16

Fishing for Urchin 18

Twice As Old 20

Glossary 22

For More Information 23

Index 24

Boldface words appear in the glossary.

Ocean Urchins

Sea urchins live in oceans all over the world. But red sea urchins are special. Scientists once thought they lived only 7 to 15 years. But these ocean animals can live 100 years—and maybe even twice that!

Red sea urchins are a species, or kind, of **marine** animal called an echinoderm. Echinoderms are invertebrates, which means they don't have a backbone—or any bones! Red sea urchins are found on the West Coast of North America, from Mexico to Alaska.

RED SEA URCHIN HABITATS

Alaska

CANADA

Oregon

California

UNITED STATES

Test and Spines

Instead of bones, red sea urchins have an outer body part called a test. It's made of 10 plates that are fused, or joined, together. Long **spines** stick out of the test. These help keep the urchin safe from **predators** and help it move across the seafloor.

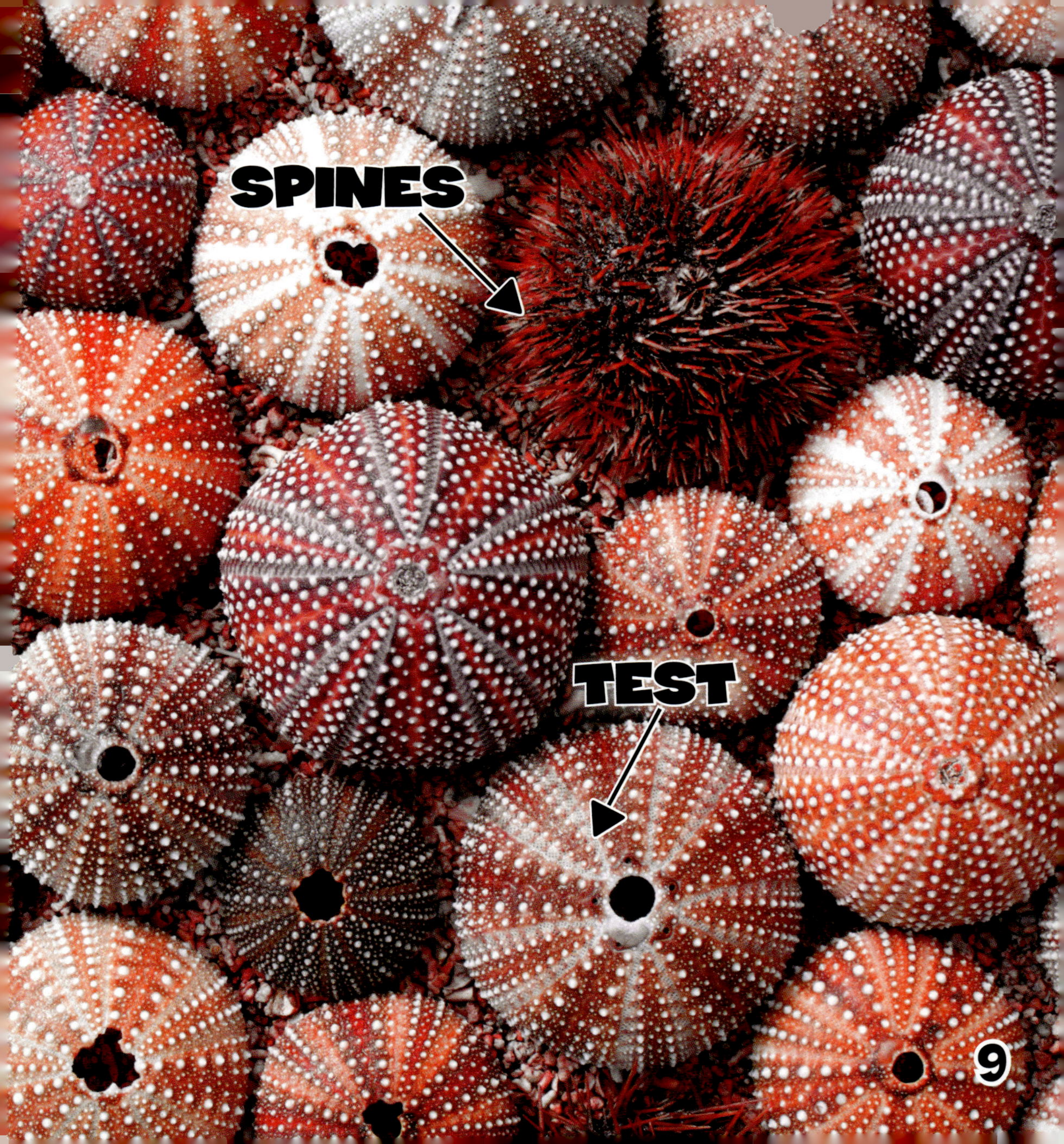
SPINES
TEST

Big Red

Red sea urchins are the largest urchins ever found. Their tests can grow more than 7 inches (18 cm) wide, and their spines can be more than 3 inches (8 cm) long! Scientists think they never stop growing, though growth slows a lot as they age.

Using Their Feet

Red sea urchins live in **shallow** waters. They like living on the rocky ocean floor and stay away from muddy areas with bits of matter called sediment. Urchins use water inside their body to move their tubelike feet.

Time to Feed

Red sea urchins eat seaweed and kelp, which are types of **algae**. Their mouth is on the bottom of their test. A red sea urchin mouth has five sharp teeth. Many red sea urchins live together to eat all the seaweed in one area!

MOUTH
TEETH

One Big Eye

Scientists think the red sea urchin body acts like one big eyeball. They use their feet and spines to move around, but the feet also have parts that can sense light. The rest of their body blocks other light so urchins can "see" what's happening right around them.

Fishing for Urchin

In the 1960s, people thought red sea urchins hurt sea life because they eat lots of kelp. They tried to **poison** them! Later, though, people began to fish for them. Sea urchin is a popular food in Japan.

SEA URCHIN

Twice as Old

In 2003, scientists learned that if red sea urchins can stay healthy and away from predators and fishing, they can live 200 years! Today, some people worry overfishing may hurt red sea urchin **populations**. We need to help these animals stay safe!

GLOSSARY

algae: plantlike living things that are mostly found in water

marine: having to do with the ocean

poison: something put into a body that causes illness or death

population: the total number of something living in an area at a given time

predator: an animal that hunts other animals for food

shallow: not deep

spine: one of many stiff, pointed parts growing from an animal

FOR MORE INFORMATION

BOOKS

Siwanowicz, Igor. *Animals Up Close: Zoom in on the World's Most Incredible Creatures.* New York, NY: Sandy Creek, 2014.

Stewart, Melissa. *Why Are Animals Red?* Berkeley Heights, NJ: Enslow Elementary, 2009.

West, Krista. *Echinoderms: Sea Stars, Sea Urchins, Sea Cucumbers, and Their Relatives.* New York, NY: Chelsea House, 2012.

WEBSITES

Red Sea Urchin
aquariumofpacific.org/onlinelearningcenter/species/red_sea_urchin
Read more about red sea urchins here.

Red Sea Urchins
marinebio.org/species.asp?id=45
Find out where red sea urchins live and more at this site.

INDEX

algae 14

echinoderms 6

eyeball 16

invertebrates 6

Japan 18

kelp 14, 18

marine animal 6

mouth 14

North America 6

oceans 4

overfishing 20

predators 8, 20

seaweed 14

species 6

spines 8, 10, 16

teeth 14

test 8, 10, 14

tubelike feet 12, 16

WORLD'S LONGEST-LIVING ANIMALS

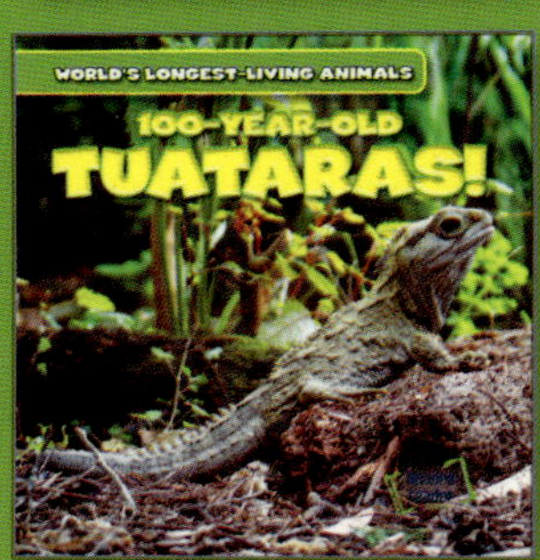

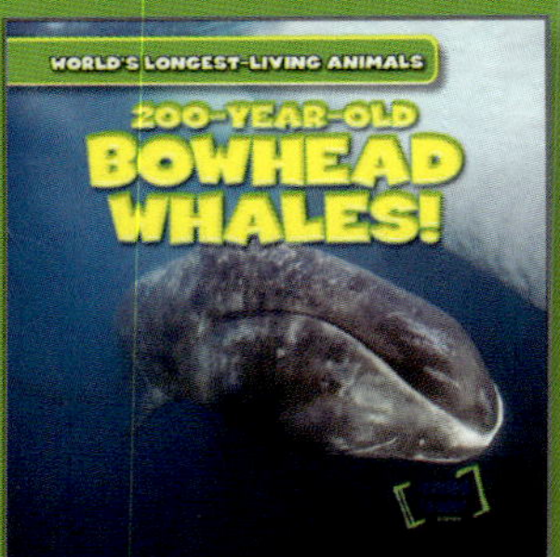

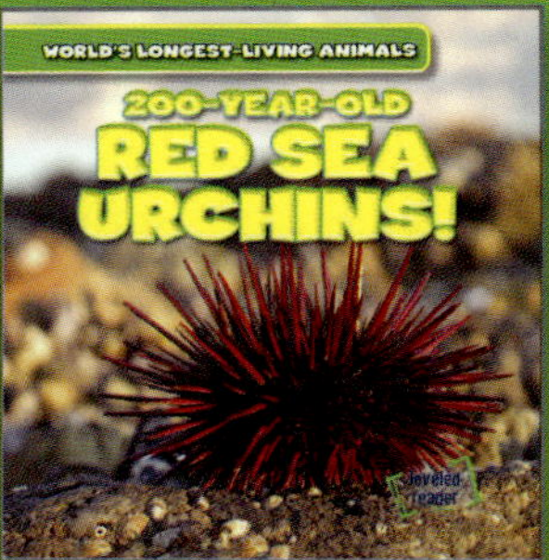

Levels: GR: H;
DRA: 14

ISBN: 9781482456394
6-pack ISBN: 9781482456417
9 781482 456394

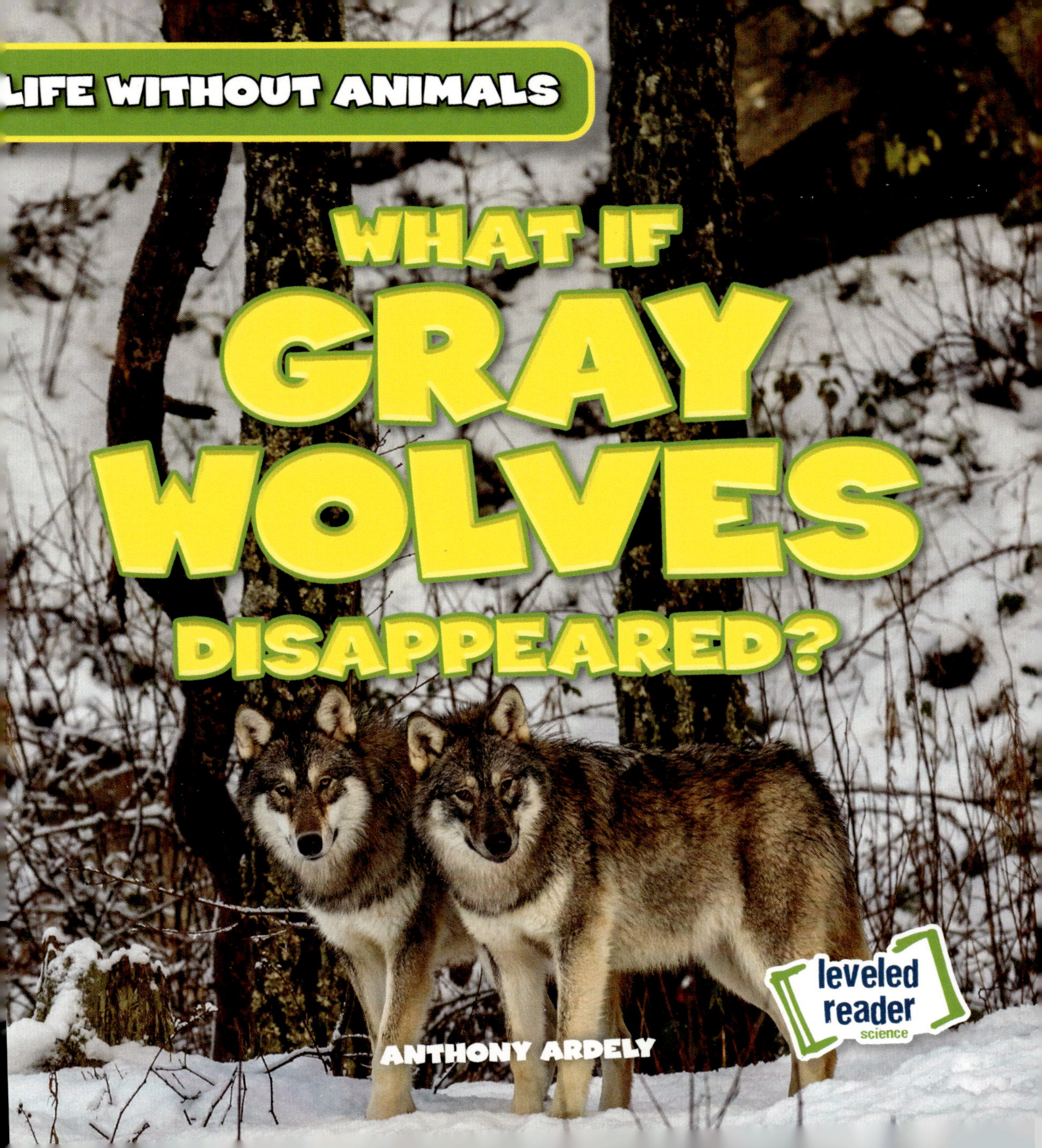
LIFE WITHOUT ANIMALS
WHAT IF
GRAY
WOLVES
DISAPPEARED?
leveled
reader
science
ANTHONY ARDELY